If there is only one thing to do well in this life,

It is to love well;

For if there is anything you are to be judged by

It is the plainness, of your loving.

— Megan E. Hoffman

www.MeganEHoffman.com

Follow *@megehoffman* on Instagram, TikTok, Twitter, Threads, and Facebook

Biting Thorns
Off Roses

Biting Thorns Off Roses

Megan E. Hoffman

Library of Congress Control Number: 2023908979
ISBN-13: 979-8-218-20808-0

Cover and Illustrations by: Megan E. Hoffman
Publisher: Megan E. Hoffman; Los Angeles, California

For all those lost inside a dark place;

The womb is also dark,

And transformative

||

Contents

Introduction

I   don't   like   feeling   stuck.

My energy very quickly coagulates, and I get antsy. As if I'm in some sort of indefinable funk, and everything I do only propels me deeper into motionless, useless frustration.

And I think, for the most part, I have felt stuck and directionless for some time. So I came up with whatever I could to distract from that feeling: reinventing myself, doom scrolling, Netflix, drugs, relationships, sex, shopping— there really are endless options.

But I think, at the end of all that, we are still left with ourselves and our dissatisfactions. And those are what we really need to dig into—get brutally honest with ourselves about—if we're ever going to be happy.

And, I think maybe I always knew that, but I was too scared to do it. Lucky for me, I'm not one to shy away from hard work indefinitely.

It took me a long time—and a very rough relationship—to finally come to a place of realizing there was never anywhere to go, except through the sludge. Because I could run forever, and that same sludge would still be there, waiting for me to find my way through it. Tossing itself up and ruining every good thing I managed to hold—until I put on the gloves, got down on my hands and knees, and started scrubbing.

So anyway, here we are; scrubbing.

It's hard to know for certain where to start, or how to direct your journey. I think the biggest learning curve for me was just in showing up as often as *I felt* I could, and allowing the path to turn in whatever direction it was going to turn that day. I'm a huge control freak, you see; so letting go and trusting can feel almost impossible.

And now I'm putting this out into the world, without a single clue of what will happen in the aftermath. Scary.

This book was as much of a journey for me as I hope it may be for you. When I started, I had a billion ideas and plans for what it 'should be'; it turned out to be none of those. But somewhere in the middle, I realized there was a theme I kept returning back to; hope.

And 'hope' is actually the very last word I wrote.

Seems fitting.

What this did turn into is a deep exploration of love; the brutality of it, the pitfalls of attachment, loyalty, and what it all means. It is a young woman wrestling with herself on some of life's biggest open-ended questions; searching for guidance, purpose, and peace.

How do we accept the unacceptable? The unfathomable? Violation of the inviolable?

Maybe hope is the only thing we can lean into, in the face of complete hopelessness;

Maybe hope, is our human superpower.

Part One

"I was searching for a vocabulary with which to make sense of death, to find a way to begin defining myself and inching forward again."
(Kalanithi, 148)*

"Until you make the unconscious conscious, it will direct your life and you will call it fate."
Carl G. Jung

There is no hope here
That fire has been extinguished;

Just let it go.

Other people were designed to break your heart.

Let it go, let it go

Hope is a stubborn and resilient thing isn't it
It will drag your weak and tired body across the
coals
Again and again and again;

It holds on

Sometimes, I wish I knew how to kill it.

||

My uncle showed up at death's door last year

Cold, tired, and alone
After forty-six winters walking around
Carrying this heavy thing on his back

I may not have much knowledge of the world
yet
But I do know that we need to change;

We don't often hold each other well.

"

I won't spend much time talking about him

In part, because all I knew of him was passed
down from others' mouths;
From a family divided

Except, I did hear his creativity could color an
entire room in warmth;

Then again, you can imagine the things you'd
say about your loved ones

And I'm sure they'd be the same;

We are only soul

"

Pride is easy to accept, in the way that it shines;

But if I asked you to join me in the dark,
   would you set down your own light, so you
could better hear me?

And what if I told you things you didn't like?
What if I said things that made you feel in ways
you'd rather not?

Would you sit still, and could you bear it?

Or would you turn away;
   would you reach for the light?

II

The rest of the world was happy
 and light-hearted;

I stood apart from that

I paint my nails black
I stand outside your walls
And I scratch, scratch, scratch

I'm waiting for the day my mind goes away
I'm waiting for the day it all goes away;

I go away.

And I have been looking for forgiveness,
but forgiveness never came;

I stand outside your walls
I paint them
Black, black, black

And now, red
The color of my bloodied, black nails

There's red on your walls!
There's red on your walls!

And you smile;
Red, red, red.

Loving you black
Splitting me in two

There's the you I can't get enough of
And the you I can't get away from;

It is only one or the other.
…

There is an absence of light,
And I've been dragged in by the hair;

Though I'll admit,
It's unclear which of us did the dragging

We melt so entirely,
I could forget to notice, when I'm hurled back.
…

I never used to be this black

Now I'm darker than you'll ever be
And you are too scared to go there;

You should be.

But you wish you didn't have a fuck to give,
Like I don't.

…

Leave me, baby—it's alright.

I lick you up like cyanide
And you make it taste so sweet;

Love me black, baby.

You never could stay, anyway
But you just can't stay away

So it's alright; we can be done tonight.

Why don't you nail me to the floor, some more
Baby
Baby
Baby

Just please;

Please, come here—
I promise we'll be alright.

‖

You'll *level* me with your disgust.

And plead for me to stay
In the same breath
…

It is here I always return
Impaled against her hollow chest,

And that warm smile

"

Stay, you'll beg
Stay—

This was your life.

...

You never wanted me to leave you;

Now, it seems the worst parts of you,

Will never leave me.

||

Somehow, I became
Responsible

For you choosing not to live

For your inadequacies, your mistakes,
Your emotions, your petty fucking grudges;

I cannot hold anything
of   my   own

My emotions
My love
my stuff

Any ground I begin to feel
Is mine
You remind me,

Can be taken away.

"

How can you *still* not see?

You strapped burdens to frames that
Did not yet have the strength to carry;

You buried us before we were dead.

‖

I was told fresh flowers and a clean living space
might help;

So I bought the flowers and I hired the cleaning
lady
…

I don't always like the stuff that I have to write
about

But I have to write it.

"

I am *terrified* of you
Every day

And it's best to slink about; keep your head
down

Count your blessings if the screams aren't at
you—

Just stay out of it; don't open your mouth.
…

Tiptoe tiptoe;
Another bad day, like all the rest;

Your depression pervades the air we breathe;

I fucking hate this house.

I hear you call, my stomach drops;
My name feels ugly in your mouth.

Tiptoe, tiptoe;
One eye on you, the other on the ground.
…

Smashed up windows
Smashed up windows

Walk on the glass, and don't complain;

I lied to my favorite teacher today
About pretty blues
Your rings left up my face.

Nobody knows and nobody sees
'You're wonderful; so involved!' they'll all say

And when they notice, they'll *still* look away;

They're all afraid, I think.

...

I turned on *family*, for you.

And they never knew why—
Do you know what that's like?

Not that I dare admit I'm upset
Because loving them, is *betraying* you.

If letting them go was the only way you would
stay;

I had to—I *needed* you.

But you better believe I still hate you
For forcing me to choose.
...

You humiliate me.

Left and right.

And never miss the chance to tell me why—

I'm the evil one;
You hope I drown in the tub

And Yet

You Still Demand
Respect.
Protection.

And My Silence.
. . .

Well, don't you worry;
The dreams still keep me screaming.

"

Cut two inches off the stems, at a forty-five
degree angle;
They'll absorb nutrients better this way

Prune any leaves too close to the bottom;
To prevent rot

Choose the *right* kind of container;
Clean, and spacious

And fill this with fresh warm water, once
every day
To avoid bacteria

Slow down wilting with a few drops of vodka;

Tip the cleaning lady

"

You asked me, once
If it was all really you, this whole time

And those tears I'd come to know so well
Came pouring down your cheeks

And I'd scooped you up into my arms,
Like a broken child;

I just didn't know any better.

But I do hope that maybe now, at least,
You finally have your answer.

||

I'm feeling disconnected
And it's freezing in here

All the time

Because life feels so heavy

And I don't feel like I have anyone to talk to
about that.

...

I feel too much to communicate.

Trapped in unsolvable mazes, set by you
Though it's never your fault, and we're all crazy;
It's true

And I know you'll never admit it,
But can we just be real for one minute;

I was always going to lose.

...

I fought so hard to keep you,
And I failed.

I fought so hard to save you,
And I failed.

24

"

I blinked hard and twenty-five years, gone by;
I want to crawl out of this skin.

Do you ever feel too much, too sad;
Too *human*, for anyone to deal with you?

A broken toy, no one would ever actually
choose?

But fuck it; what the fuck do I know—
I'm sure I just sound silly.

"

It's the shadow chasing you
That makes looking in the mirror so hard

It is the deepest part of your spirit they stole;
The one that still follows you around like
a pathetic puppy, begging

No matter how hard you try to cut it out
No matter how many different directions you
look

It sits; it waits;
It steeples its fingers

It waits to remind you that you do not belong to
yourself;

That you still belong to, somebody else.

"

They say time heals, but in my experience
Time does nothing unless you make use of it;

Come to terms with the wreckage
Make it livable

Allow it to breathe
…

Each improperly healed bone must break again,
To be reset.

||

I have a story to tell

And a difficult decision in how to approach
telling it
…

I think I've just been so angry.

And now, sitting next to all these pages
With all this anger spewed over them, I realize—

This is not how *I* want to be;
It's not the story I wish to tell.

But then, what kind of story should it be?

"

I can say that something went wrong
And now my world is very tight; controlled

I could play high and mighty, and tell you that,

"Well, we should all aim to grant others the
same acceptance for their humanness, that we
deserved when we needed it"

And that may be true; but it feels like bullshit.

Or, I can tell you of all the things I cannot
put down
Or will not put down

And that I would like to write a story of
forgiveness

But I think that would be a lie because, well
I haven't found it yet.

But that, too, has to be okay, I think.

"

Snow blanketed the ground the night I ran out
the door so fast,
I hadn't had time for shoes

And the sobs broke through my determination
As the wet and the ice soaked through my socks;

I couldn't feel my feet
And we both knew I had nowhere to go

So you laughed as I swallowed my personhood
back down to the pit,

And turned around;

Not a single porch light came on.
…

Snow poured from the sky through the long and
freezing hours I waited

For you to come get me

For you to finish the lesson of degradation being
frozen to my bones

So lasting, I can still feel the cold.
…

And there were piles of snow I sunk knee-deep
into

The night I snapped

And jumped out the window, and hauled my
pack

And ran and trudged while more snow dumped
itself overhead

I made it to the road
Praying
For willpower, for speed;

Praying you'd not notice till I was already gone.

"

My friend.

You had been my hero, once.

And you had been the sweetest of all my things,
once.

And I could not break myself from loving you,
Any more than I could break myself from
eating, or from drinking

But this thing you gave me—it's a half life;
It's an icy, and a frozen life
Shattered again and again and again;

My friend.

And still, though my body is warm now
It is so often I find myself,

barely breathing

So.

What now

How do I do this

And if what I need, cannot be you

What should it be?

Today, I'll let you know
A little boy called me,
Courageous

I told him how I left
And his eyes got wide

And   how   scared   you
must   have   been,

Left his lips

As I sneak around the place
to pick the things I will need and,

What I Will Miss

And my heart empties out
As I seethe with fear
And backbone
And once I start I
Cannot Fail

    And Courageous, is a funny word

        When it's mixed with
         so   much   grief.

I know I've been away a long while

I tend to live in my head;
                                   people are lovelier there

I don't know when I stopped taking the time to
pause at beautiful views

I don't know when I stopped making the effort
to seek them out
…

Pain does twist so many things, don't you think?

And have you, too, noticed how all anger
is really fear

        Or are you, also, too prideful to admit that?
                                                    …

I can say, this world is a lot for me to take in,
And maybe I don't always believe I belong to it;

I think, sometimes, tired is less a feeling
And more a personality trait.

And maybe I wish they would have told me
before I got here;

Who'd have thought there'd be such a heavy
price to pay for your own life—

Carrying the weight of a heart.

If Anger could speak, it would beg to be seen
It would scream and scream until it's throat gave
out—

"Fight for my life!";

I was a burdened child
And not much about that has changed.

If Grief had a voice
It would sound like a little girl,
Carrying the weight of a life held too close to
her bones;

Of love like coffee stained teeth.

The lives we have lived deserve proper funerals
But the putting to rest;

That, my dear friend, is the beast.

||

Maybe I put my *heart*, into the wrong people;
Certain ones have a knack for extinguishing
hope

But I cannot believe they mean to do it

"

Your world is impossible to untangle
And you have made everyone I love, sad

Not just sad. *Broken-spirited.*

How many tender things have you held in your
hands
And smothered

How does one forgive that?

"

Faces change, but time does not do much for you
My friend

Yours is the cup that remains empty.

I wish, I wish, I knew how to fill it.

Isn't it a funny feeling; guilt
And the things we feel it for

I'm not sure which is harder; being unloved
Or being taught love is what it isn't

But both leave you robbed

And angry.

"

It took me two decades to understand,
You never knew how;
Yours came with strings of compliance attached

And obligatory love is a piss poor excuse for it.

"

I left, I left
And still the guilt came;

That unwanted visitor, who refuses to leave.

||

I believe I have loved you well

Or at least, to the best of my ability;
You've not made it easy

What a test to see how many times I could crack
And stitch myself back
With you

It still did not pan out;
But that is the honest way of it
Isn't it

...

Have I told you of religion

Have I not shown you how I pray
Down on both knees with my hands clasped,
To You

But You, do not pray back;
You never pray back

Why don't you pray back?

||

There isn't much to this life that feels very real
to me

And maybe you'll label *that* a disorder—
Go ahead; I'm sure I've collected a few.

Someone once told me that I am an,
'out of sight, out of mind,' kind of person.

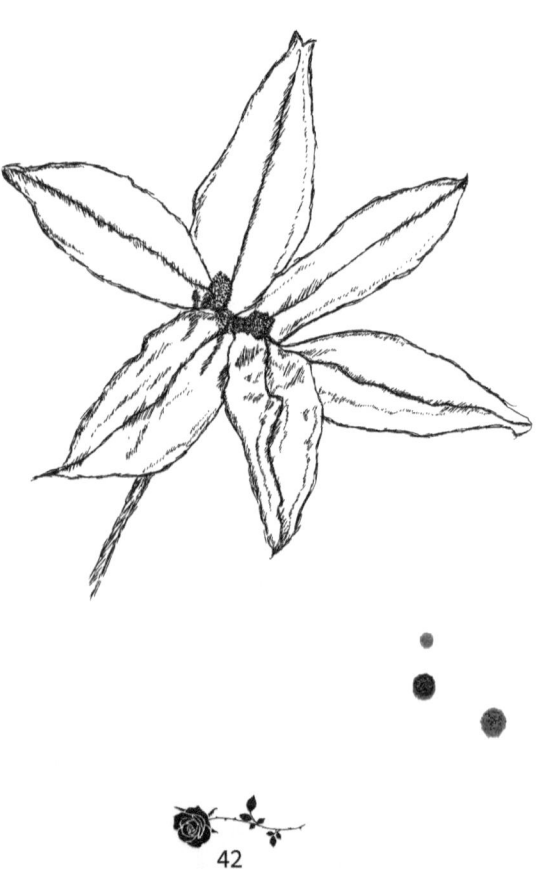

"

Time is a funny thing

And it's hard really, to ever be certain of
how I feel,

    Or of how I felt

More than likely, the thought of you will harass
my heart in those same old painful ways
I'll never make sense of

    So. I guess I'll just leave it at that.

‖

I've made a habit of shutting down feelings and
pulling the mental plug;

I think I've scared people with that;
I think I've hurt myself with that;

I don't bond easily.

Intimacy is ever changing;
You either allow the world to see you in new,
more raw, fractured lights

Or you don't;

I usually opt for the latter.

"

I've never been the best speaker

My emotions roll over my words till my body is
hot, and trembling
And before I know it, I'm forgetting myself
Tripping over my own fat tongue;

I think it makes me look stupid.

I am not stupid.

44

It takes a lot for me to feel safe;
I almost never do,
So I'm quiet.
...

I don't know how to express the shame I feel
over that

So I'll just write it down and hope that as you
read it,
And I'm not forced to look you in the eyes

You'll understand exactly what I mean.
...

Tiptoe, tiptoe
One eye on the ground, the other on all of you;

I'm scared
I'm scared
I'm scared

...

I don't know how to make it stop.

||

45

You see an unmade bed

Dirty dishes in the sink and laundry strewn
across the floor;
I see mountains of indecision

Do you know what you want?

And have you sat alone in the dark just to see
what comes up?

I wonder if you've felt how fulfillment feels, and
if so
Could you maybe share it with me?

Not so I could steal it, or any silly thing like that
But so I, too, can know what the world is
supposed to feel like

Maybe then I'd finally find the energy to do things

Like making beds and washing dishes and folding laundry.

On betrayal.
…

I imagine the thought of us having needs and
desires apart from yours, must perplex you

Because your wants, are automatically ours, too;

I don't think you see much outside of that.

And like puppets on strings;
I don't think you see us, outside of you.

"

Did you want to keep me alone, and afraid?

Or maybe small, and helpless;

Why did you so badly need me, to need you?
…

You know, I believed every word you ever told
me

And I never thought you would be like this;

I never could have even imagined
…

What, the fuck, happened here?

"

First of all
Let me remind you—

This is love;
Not charity.

"

And second; I have felt responsible

But there is a guilt, and a fear
Accompanying powerlessness,

Thick as cold, hard molasses—

Until we accept it

"

What does *love* dictate
That we owe?

There's something tugging at my mind
An unsettled feeling;

> *a burning compulsion to understand*

Obsession may be the downfall of me,
Or the black light

…

I am gestating

The things everyone else has stopped talking
about

> still hold great weight in my mind

I've been pulled away and cocooned in this dark
place for some time;

All there is to do is wait

"

Trauma separates

And there is a shame that follows; one I did not
see coming
Listeners mean well but they never say the right
things

...and it hurts to hear the wrong things.

Our world lacks an effective empathetic
vocabulary;

                    I hope with my whole heart
                        we can change that

"

So much time I've spent wondering at what is
normal and what is not

And then I've wondered at who we are to say
I write to give you that validation;
                        I write to give it to myself

The world is quick to open its mouth
And slow to sit in the dark place, to understand
why it is dark

                        It is fear;
                    It is ignorance;
                It is weakness of the heart.

                                    ||

The things I wish I knew how to say to you
…

The people we love, pose the greatest challenges.

                                                    ”

                        We don't talk.
                        And I wish we did.

I don't know how to communicate how much
I feel for you
Or how much I feel, because of you;

And now some of you are dead.
…

            And this is a really difficult piece to write.

"

So much of this time is hazy
And I don't think I ever really knew what was
going on

All I know is how much I wanted to keep you
And I couldn't.

                    And that I never told you that.

And that I failed.

...

Maybe the most clear, concise thing I can say
simply, is

I miss you.

So, so much.

I love you.

So, so much.

And I'm sorry.

‖

I got out

I got out, and You didn't.

I got out
And now I get to Heal, and Expand, and Thrive
While you still only just survive

And that's not fair.

And it's not right.

And I wish I could change it
But I can't.
…

What I would give
To have known, at the time,
That I should have taken you, too

What I would give
To have known that I should have fought
For You

With every bone in my body
And every breath in my lungs

I should have fought;

But I didn't know how

I still don't know how.

...

To the sweetest little girl to ever walk the earth—

You deserved so much more
So much more than any of us could give you

You came in, and you brought your light
And your life
And your sparkle

And your love;

And this world;
It just took that from you;

Didn't it.

And there isn't anything in the world I can say
that would bring it back
…

Is there.

"

I didn't know, at the time, what was going on

Or who was the threat
…

And I need to apologize for not protecting you
properly;

And to tell you that if there was anything in this
life I could take back,

It would be that

"

And if I had a pony

And a castle

And a rich, handsome prince at my disposal

And something about a pair of wings to pick
you up

And fly you far, far away from here

and

and you know

I'm honestly not even sure how to end this one.

...

So.

I guess I'll just leave it at that.

||

"He who knows not that the Prince of Darkness is the other face of the King of Light, knows not me."
Manly P. Hall

"That which sings and contemplates in you, is still dwelling within the bounds of that first moment, which scattered the stars into space. Who among you does not feel that his power to love is boundless?"
Kahlil Gibran

You know
I can be pretty damn self-righteous

Sometimes.
...

The kind of self-righteous that angers when
I pour my heart into someone,
And they refuse to listen

And I think I've been afraid to reach out
because, well
I feel I need to be less of those things, first;

I don't want to keep messing this up.
...

I expected all the things a daughter, sister, friend,
or lover
Should be able to expect

But I also forgot that 'should be', isn't always
'what is'

And that 'what is', is usually the thing we most
don't want to accept.

So I refused

And I got rigid;
And I turned cold;
And I hardened;

I boarded up my heart.

"

It is far easier to be angry, and right
Than broken and sad

And I was honestly trying to help
But you know how I get when I believe
I know best

What is the road they say is paved with
good intentions?

…

And I couldn't walk in your shoes
And I wouldn't meet you where you stood

And I see now, that none of this really even
mattered anyway,

Because I could be the most righteous person in
the world

And in this case, I'd still be wrong;

I'd still be wrong.

||

What draws me in, to this?

Is it love, or something twisted—
Said a mother to her daughter
It's so hard to tell the difference

        But please;
            I need to know the difference

"

I didn't understand then
And I won't pretend to know much more now;
All I can do is try to not be angry

        And at that, I'll fail.

            But I'll learn

"

I used to believe in the world, with an innocent
infatuation for its goodness

    Now I believe, with a knowing compassion for
its faults

    ...

I think things that are perfect are easy to love;

    We meet God in our love for that which is not

‖

67

Surrender

…

I am intense, to say the least
But I had to turn away;

Some things are just too heartbreaking to keep
looking.

"

How to let a thing go

The very thing that's been glued—fused to your
bones

As substantial as the food you eat,
Necessary as the air you breathe

No, I don't think I'm there yet;

But I've been trying to be

And honestly, I don't know which will win out in
the end;

My love, or my resentment.

But I do hope it is the former

And if there is anything I believe in, it is hope

"

Can't anyone tell me;
Where is the forgiveness point?

||

It is easier to get mad,

Than to seek understanding;

Easier to be cold and focused, than terrified;

Easier to label it shame, than trauma.

||

Do you think the world fears pain?

When the animals sense the reaper coming to
collect their dues

Do you think they fight, beg, and bargain
for their lives?

Or do they open their arms in mighty
gratitude—

Thank you for this borrowed time

"

I wonder what comes to Your mind when You
think of strength

Is it survival?

Is it pushing through the pain at all costs

Digging in your heels
and refusing

to be torn apart

Or

Is it sitting in the dark with an open heart?

Willing to hear what *ache* has to say

Willing to be moved; willing to die;

Willing to be reborn

"

If you asked me some time ago what strength
meant

I might have whole-mindedly preached the first
definition;

Now I think—I hope—I'm coming to trust
wholeheartedly, in the second

||

How to move forward when the world stops.

I'll admit I haven't quite figured this one out yet,
But I feel it must have something to do with
b r e a t h i n g

"

Why is it that the deepest pain withdraws

Why does the most profound torment hide
in the thickest silence

Offering its grief like bread; you could slice it
with a knife
And what will be the butter?

I wonder; is the pen mighty enough
to soothe an ache like that?

"

And tell me;

If you woke one day without that weight
strapped to your back

If you felt the space in the broad expanse of
your shoulders

The uprightness of your spine

And your lungs o p e n e d
                          Like a flower turned towards
                                              the sun

                    Please God, tell me;
            What would you do with a day like that?

‖

When the time calls for it
You must *allow* your heart,
to break

           "

Daddy.

Can you see me now?

There's so much I've been needing to tell you,
But I didn't know how.

Are you there; are you listening?

Mommy says she's not feeling well.

And I've been waiting for her to come,
But she stays away now;

She goes to sleep on the couch.

Now her hair has gone dull, and her skin sallow
All her bones are poking out and her jeans
just fall down

...

Daddy
I don't know what to do.

"

There is a nightmarish, inhuman figure;
A great and unreasonably cruel beast—

It's taken her now.

Daddy, please tell me;
Are you there?

And will you help get her out?

"

Sound cannot exist without air
And this terror of a thing has sucked up the
whole house

Have you ever screamed until your lungs burst,
And not made a single sound?

She's choking; she's not breathing;
And now, it's pulled a knife out.

It's shrieking and sobbing and crawling up to
her room
Now it's closing the door;

Daddy, I don't think she's coming back out.

I don't know what to do

I don't know what to do

Please help me!

Daddy, just make her calm down!

"

But you weren't there, were you?

Daddy, are you still listening?
And will you sit with me now?

If I tell you something you wouldn't like
If I said things that made you feel in ways
you'd rather not

Would you stay; and could you bear it?

And would you save us this time around?

II

Tell me, what do you carry in your mind
That makes your spirit heavy?

And does this world make you tired?

And the animals, the ones that mate for life;
Do you think there's all this hemming and
hawing over who to be with

Or, do they just
                        know

"

I've said goodbye so many times
But I don't think I've ever done it right;

To love a mortal thing with
                        all of yourself

To hold it against your bones like breath

Like food, like water

And to let it go when it asks to be free

Trusting that its substance will neither be
diminished nor destroyed;

Yes, that's it—trust; that is the tricky part.

Tell me; do you release love willingly
Or is it *ripped* from your bones

Does it leave gaping holes in your skin
Does it leave you bedridden for weeks, months,
even years at a time

Unable to mend your broken, heavy life?

"

And yet I swear, I see myself staring back
through your eyes

Is that alone not proof enough, for trust;
for faith?

||

81

I do much enjoy the life of a poet
And I believe it fits me well

No one would ever have to pay me
To wander through the openings and enclosures
of my mind

Or to explore the depths of my very ordinary
soul;

I do this naturally, and often.

But it is the sharing that scares me;

I doubt anyone knows the sensitivity I carry
Or the dramatism with which I am capable of
expressing it—

But there I go again, invaliding my own self.

I'll be the first to say, I don't understand it;

What is wrong with vulnerability, and why is it
so hard to share it?

I think at times, I lead too much with this silly,
judgemental mind;

I think at times, we'd learn so much
from our wise, and very ordinary souls.

||

What is it in this life that brings you peace;

And have you given yourself over to it?

Or does ambition tear you away,
Does it eat at the corners of your mind
Like a ravenous thing;
Greed and power
Those unquenchable thirsts—

What will you make of your life?

Must you make anything?

I won't pretend to know much, but I will say this;
I've felt more peace meandering through fields
talking to flowers
Than I have in all the cities filled with all the
industrial promise in the world

What a funny breed we humans are, don't you think?

I wonder if we'll ever learn to just,
let a thing be

||

Did you notice her eyes
When offered a simple, how are you?

She's been standing all night behind
that counter
And no one has paid any mind.

Did you watch his face as he held up his sign
Begging for tiny bites of affection;

They all, every single one,

turned their heads.

…

Have *things* stuffed your ears, and covered your
eyes?

"

Have you wondered at the reason why?

Do you think there is one, at least some of the
time
And have you ever let that reason, or lack
thereof,

Consume you

"

I hope my words find better footing when
I'm older;

I am young,
Carrying the arrogance that youth does

Hubris had me convinced, with enough
determination
I might make the world turn at my speed

Humility takes time and, perhaps
a certain number of beatings.

"

Are we the lucky ones then
With our money and our things,
and our too busy lives?

In another world, a toothless man squats
by the Ganges
Amidst all the disease and the squalor
Smiling as he gives up his only shoes
to a stranger;

And do you wonder why?

...

How are you, friend—
Really?

And do you know what will carry us through
this life?
Because it so does seem that something is
missing;

Something very, *very* important

||

I wonder how many times I'll rewrite the pages
of my life

> before I am satisfied;

Is the mind just a sieve to keep pouring into
and never be filled?

And what is ambition anyway, if not for the
sake,

> of satisfaction?

…

Small flower
Gentle flower

> Do you know why you are here?
> And do you already know where you are going?

You must know, I think

For you never try to get to any place other than
where you are

You do not toil away at desks in enclosed spaces
pondering your purpose—

Do you?

It doesn't seem so;

    I think lives lived in surety must be peaceful.

So, in the case of soul—

If I am you, little flower, and you are me

Tell me;

      What is keeping me from knowing
                what you know?

Thank you for this great, and all-consuming
task—
My life

I haven't made peace with it yet;
I don't even make my bed in the morning

But I am trying

 My God, I promise; I am trying.

I've been in this body for twenty-five years
And I have to say;

I thought I would've been farther along by now.

I honestly didn't expect to have to deal with *any*
of this
...

I've tried on many faces

Painted over instability with the brush
of ambition
But I think it's time to take the masks off now—

I'm just too young to feel so old

"

There's a happy soul waiting in the wings

She's waiting to remind you of something
you've forgotten:

That maybe we have nowhere to be

And I think, maybe, I've lived many better lives
in my sleep

But there's still something about *this* world
That makes me want

to dream

||

Yes, I would say I'm obsessive;

Look, in my eyes there are two mindsets
When it comes to defining success—

The first is the willingness to trade your days,
For a sense of security

And the second is the Determination to sacrifice
everything,

For your *Freedom;*

Whatever I come to be in this life,
Let me fall into the latter category.

‖

Why ever do anything at all for ambition;
What kind of silliness is that?

But deep, *unyielding* enjoyment—

The only thing worth every penny in your
pocket;

Every last inch of your bones.

Things I love;
Sleepy old beach towns that smell like salt

Soft, early morning light

The screech of gulls outpouring into the sunrise,
swooping across that streaked sky

And how you can see them,
                                even with your eyes closed

Being home;

How that crisp air makes you want to pull on a
too-big sweater, and cozy up with a book

The steaming mug of something hot,
resting close

Home smells like musk, and pine
With a tinge of campfire smoke

It sounds like secret birds singing brightly from
their perches;

They'll go all day, but the best
                are their fervent praises before the sun

They do not need the light to know when it is
time to give thanks;

You can smell it coming, in the dew rising off the
grasses
                    bathing the air with its wetness

And speaking of grass;

Have your ever paused to notice how all a dog
needs to be content in this world,
                    Is an emerald patch of grass?

How they'll drop and roll their backs in the
blades for hours upon hours,

Sloppy tongues dangling out of wide, lazy smiles

And have you ever taken a moment to wonder
Just what that might mean?

Maybe absolutely nothing;

                    But also, maybe *everything*

If there is only one thing you hold close to
your heart

Let it be softness;

        This life cannot be forced

      Like the mind, when it finally learns to cease its
                     endless chatter

      And the body, as it withers on its way back to
                     the soil

.

All things come
in their own time;

So will the healing

‖

To love, is a funny thing;

The world does it wholly, and with ease
But us humans have our rules,

Our silly minds that must make the senseless,
sensible

But, I wonder if this doesn't rob us
of the meaning;

You wouldn't shrink the universe down into a
cup just so you could look at it,

                                        Would you?

                                            ||

Learning to hold others
without judgment

Is, perhaps
the most valuable skill we have to cultivate

I   feel   like   I   should   say   what   I   mean,
when   I   talk   to   God

Yes, let me be more specific—
I wouldn't want anyone to assume I meant some
robed, bearded figure

Or that I'd ever call God, Him;

Though if that's what you'd prefer,
that's your business

In a way, I suppose, I'm only speaking to my
wiser self

    Which is also the wiser self present in every
           human, well as it may be hidden

But sometimes I'll ask the trees or the animals
Who—I believe—are a bit more in touch

If you cannot sense the God in the mighty give
of the ocean

Or in the sturdy earth beneath your feet
I wish, I wish,

    You'd   only   take   off   your   shoes

‖

If there is one thing I question
It is to whom I owe allegiance

Countries
Politics
Wars
Races
Divisions
Boundary lines

It is all the same;

History repeats, and this is neither the end nor
the beginning.

I know I am white, and this speaks privilege

But more than I am white, I am human

More than I am American
I am a visitor, come to enjoy

My foremost task: to give thanks

To this beautiful place we have, by some miracle

Been allowed to exist on from the confines of
our fleshy bodies

That same miracle we so naively strive,
To own, tame, and conquer;

Our species speaks of pain.

But the world exists in perfect love and
indifference;

It does not discriminate the man from the
woman

The African from the European
Devout from atheist
Dog from cat

Or even the grass from our own hair

Most certainly it does not separate our breath
From the free floating air—

No, this world is here to be;

And so am I.

What if we simply chose to set down

Our petty rules, arrogant identities, powers,
and thoughts;

Do we not all owe the same thanks?

I don't know.

These are only my thoughts; you can take them
or leave them

But whatever we come to be in this life
I do hope we all learn to love wholly,
and well.

||

We talk about Authenticity, Intimacy;

The world is a prayer

The real, intimate chord of humanness running
through every body,

Is how we suffer.

The real, intimate chord of Being running
through every body,

Is how we love

||

111

Soft eyes
Large and glassy

Feeling the world as you see it

Opening, through the skin,
Touching someplace deeper;

To meet a naked soul

"

I know I have felt you looking at me before

Though I don't know what color your eyes were then,
Or the shape of them

Maybe they were blue,
or green, like the sea

But all that does not matter;
Bodies are only temporary things

"

What is that, which has brought you back?

Again, no matter—

The all-important task now is, the thanking

The parting of the lips
Of the skin

The merging;

Only to be parted, again
When the time for this body comes to an end

"

To love a mortal thing with *all* of yourself

To hold it against your bones like breath
Like food, like water

And to let it go when it asks to be free

Trusting that it's substance will neither be
diminished nor destroyed;

Is this not our life's greatest work?

Some call the man who died crossing into wild
territory, naive
Others call him reckless; stupid, even

What a good and full life he might have lived
had he just,
Abided by the way of things;

By our way of things, I mean

But spirit is unbounded

Maybe you'll lay back and claim he got what
was coming to him;
Hell, maybe he did

But still,
This man who Understood—

His life of no more importance than the
mountains he climbed

Than the blades of grass outside your cozy,
confining bedroom window

This man who understood His Place,
Amongst the wild indifference of things

"

Are we not all here to teach each other, of loss?

Of cyclic, and inevitable change
And the unyielding cord of love, which binds
and frees?

I do not know much, but from what I have
gathered
The greatest lessons are still the simple, and the
timeless ones:

Be Here Now; pay *close* attention
Submit utterly, and completely

Allow love to *fill* you, to *humble* you,
To *exist* as you;

And once you have gathered this—

Give yourself to the world

||

Marc-André Leclerc
October 10, 1992 - March 5, 2018

115

Feelings come and go

The easy ones; waking up to rain outside your
bedroom window
The steaming cup of something hot, brought to
your lips

The hard ones are sticky tar caked to the bottom
of your feet
These must be scraped and scrubbed relentlessly
until they release
Oftentimes taking the skin with them;

It grows back;
Everything grows back

Through all this, the love stays the same

It may be covered, it may need to be scrubbed
and scraped
                        But itself unaltered, remains;

                        Life is not a simple thing

||

Yes, my feet are dirty;
They have walked a long ways

And this is the kind of dirt that doesn't wash
away

It cakes in the cracks and stains the soul—
This dirt is my prayer to the earth

May I meld into it, and it, into me

"

Bless me with truth, and I will show you
meaning;

Let us never leave this world, unscathed
Let us never again, be clean

Something has died;

I didn't get what I wanted.

I didn't get what I wanted

...and that is sad.

We all carry graves inside of us.

"

Have you considered that we do not grieve out
of anger,
But out of love;

And is that not more beautiful than any amount
of bitterness you could possibly carry?

"

I have held on too tight;
I have been buried with the dead thing,
  And I did it by choice

On this, I am still working

Death is an evolution if you rise to the occasion;
Be brave
Rise to it

118

"

Things have a way of reaching us more deeply,
and with greater poignance,

In their absence.

When meaning comes to slip through the cracks,

Allow it

...

There is so much to learn in your grief;

Build a temple here

Make it home

||

Mother—

You gave me darkness,

and you gave me light.

I do believe that both in their own right, are gifts,

though I will say one much harder
than the other

Then again, I've never been one to shy away from hard work.

"

I wonder, what softness will come of this?

Does one become strong by

biting the thorns off roses,

Or does that make me, a masochist?

"

There is much I deserved and still do,
though I'll never receive it

I know you begged for your life,
                          and it was not given to you

Nor did anyone show you how to take it;

                    I know that you could not give
                        what you never received.

And there is much we need to take responsibility
for;

Mending our own lives before inflicting them on
the world—
                    But then again, I do understand.

    We are not all born so lucky so as to be able
                        to do this task;

        This great, and all-consuming task.

"

I know a life that gets caught in the waves and
the undertow,

                        I know a life that lacks peace.

A child, too busy fighting to be seen;
To be saved—

And a woman

                who never learned how to see;

How to save herself.

||

123

I have wondered in the past, why me?

Which seems a silly thing to wonder really,
When the obvious answer is,

well, why not me—

I was not picked out of a profiled line up to
receive pain.

You can be angry at the world, at God, the
universe,

Or whatever it is you choose to believe in

And still, the world will respond with indifferent
silence;

I hope I'm past wasting life on pointless
questions.

"

I'll say again, I don't know much

But I do understand, that you are only asked to
listen

And if you can bring yourself to do this singular
thing,

Maybe you'll find the deeper you are pulled into
that silence
                The softer your anger becomes
                       ...

Inside this silence, that vibrates, and hums
And is maybe not so indifferent, after all;

Listen. *Listen*

              Everything has something
                 to do with

                   this

                   ||

Mind is a heavy thing; tight
It lives through a clenched fist

Love does not pry open its fingers
Love does not overstep, nor impose

But Love knows it is heard best,

                when Mind falls silent

And so Love is just there

            Waiting for Mind to start breathing

||

Yesterday is not today
Though I carry it with me; an expired bottle of
hard pills to swallow

"

I tried walking away when I became too angry
to look
I tried dropping the heavy thing on the ground
and refusing to turn back

But wouldn't you agree;
Running only draws out the torment of a life
                        not being lived as is meant

"

Small thing
Sacred thing
          Come out and open the pain of your body
                                        to me

          And this time, I will not turn away

          Share with me that great *ache* you carry
          And let's walk awhile on this beach of
                              nourishment;

                    In this deep ocean of my life

And when the time comes for you to let it all go
Small thing
Sweet thing

Will you slip the wounds from your body like silk

Like holy water

Will you smell the salt wafting through the air
And realize, finally,

that this life is for you, too?

...

So they went hand in hand, tracing the line of
the water
Giggling at some secret joke; crying over shared
history

And the birds;
They lifted their feathery bodies high into the air
Trusting their wings to carry them

Everyone, in due time, making their way back
Home

‖

Is there a place more wild, lonely, or desolate
than the human heart?

Take me to one and I might believe you,
But I doubt it

I love, I love, I love

"

That child who has not been taught how to love,
but loves still, and wholly

Without hesitation
Without rules or regulation

It loves, it loves, it loves

"

I've walked the most feral places I could find,
and felt adoration for every square inch

I've wandered the most barren spaces of my
chest, and found them surprisingly full

Have you, too, noticed how far the heart
stretches?

That lawless thing; that innocent,

defiant thing

Begging   to   wrap   itself
around   the   entire   world

And I wonder;

Who are you,

to tell a thing like that,

no?

It's easier to miss you,
Than to be near you

And if that isn't the saddest statement I've made
I don't know what is.

I love you,
And it's so damn hard to be near you;

What am I supposed to do with that?

We all make this so complicated,
You and I,

Don't we?

"

I see you as through a mirror, as myself

And make painful statements,
and ask silly questions;

But I am so sad

I know you are. And here I am.

I have been so tight, so controlled

I know you have. And here I am.

But my heart has been broken so   much   more,
                          than it has   been   whole

I know; I know it has. And here I am.

But who are you?

I am That

     I am That

         I am Them

             And I am You

                                    ...

Sat chit ananda

Balance

When there is a quiet spaciousness between
You   and   I

And   myself
and   the   world

And I can be a part of it

                    And see what's underneath,

                              Purified

                                        …

          How do we rest in the peaceful place?

"

I find such more delight in the body

Than using the mind for words

          The moment thoughts land on my tongue

          Anxiousness floods, and I lose   *this*

"

There is so much to remember;

Try not to take this life *so* seriously

This is a fun game between
You   and   I

And   myself
and   the   world;

How many levels can you play with;

How deeply can you love it all?

"

The depth to which *you love*,

Is the depth to which you meet God

I had no idea how far I had to go with it
Or the distance still to walk;

So patience becomes a friend.
…

You were born right where you needed to be

And as a result of that, other people
         With their emotions and their needs and
                              their will

         Had come to feel very painfully threatening
                              to me.

But in the wisdom of Ram Dass—
         You don't have to pretend your neuroses
                              aren't real

         Or even expect them to go away;

         Just greet them when they stop by for tea

"

There is so much anger in the world already;

People don't need to be told how to be angry,
Or self-righteous

So I've done my best not to do that

But perhaps 'what is the anger here to say'
Is a valid question
...

And 'life goes on' is the oldest cliche in the book
So I won't use it

But—
There is much more to come, after

...

Something tells me the way forward,
Is through the break,

And that as long as you try
There will be life;

And hope

"

Bring your darkness

Into your light

Not to drown out the dark

But so that they both may love,

together

With the same face

‖

I think

if I lay here long enough

Maybe I could sink into the earth

The thunder of the ocean would fill me;
possess me

Would come to take me back home

And when I wake again I'll have forgotten

who I was

And remembered

Who I Am

Yes, that's right;

    silly body,

        silly mind

I am not you,

And you are not me

But we;

    Yes   we   are

E   v   e   r   y   t   h   i   n   g

…

And someone, somewhere   is singing

||

the end

p.s. •

For *You*—

You taught me how to argue; and how to lose

                And how to apologize

To try, no matter how often I fail

            And to be brave,
                  alongside the fear

You showed me it is safe to be exactly

Who I am

And how to let the person next to me
be who they are, too

And while there are a million things I could say,
I strongly doubt any of it would be enough;

So, I suppose I'll just have to settle for *this*—

Thank you

Thank you

about the book

"Our world lacks an effective empathetic vocabulary; I hope with my whole heart we can change that"

In a way, this single line sums up the entire reason why this book came to be. I saw a tightness; a need to open up space around a deeper conversation, about trauma and the aftereffects of it.

At first, it was the loved ones I saw in pain, and myself not understanding. Next, it was the people in society whom I saw being judged—whom I myself judged, because the world couldn't feel what they were going through.

And finally, it was me.

I was the one carrying around immense, invisible suffering; and unable to understand myself.

I've watched dozens of people struggle
with deep regret. And I've noticed how many
of them felt too lost, or too helpless to help
themselves. I've watched this misunderstanding
create divides between loved ones lasting
years—and sometimes, lifetimes.

I found myself cycling through phases and
relationships, looking for something, or someone
who would be able to *see me*. And maybe I would
find healing in that.

But eventually I realized something: no one
would be able to see me. Because I couldn't *see
myself*.

With this book, I strive to find that
understanding; compassion; empathy. And to
find my starting point for communicating—
which is, perhaps, all most of us really need.

When you're alone with no one to guide you,
doing the work toward acceptance is not only
hopelessly uncertain—it's terrifying. My greatest
hope for this book is that it might help others
create space between themselves and their pain,
the way it has helped me create space in mine.

Space to b r e a t h e; to feel; to understand.

Perhaps you'll find that at the end of the day,

seeing   yourself

is   all   you   really   need.

Lovingly,

Megan Elisabeth Hoffman

*Kalanithi, Paul. *When Breath Becomes Air*. Random House Usa, 12 Jan. 2016.

about the author

Megan E. Hoffman

Is a twenty-five-year-old
Vermont native

Has a great love of nature
Lounging on empty beaches
Singing in the shower at the top of her lungs
And cruising across mountain roads
with all the windows down
headbanging to Nirvana

Is a traveler
Is a seeker of peace

She lives in Los Angeles, California
with her two beloved dogs;
Tsintah and Tahoma

Your Review Helps More Than You Know!

If this book left an impression on you in some way, please consider leaving a review on Amazon, Goodreads.com, or your favorite review site.

Thank you so much for your support as a reader;

All my love